CW01368820

NOTHING MORE

Krystyna Miłobędzka
NOTHING MORE
WIĘCEJ NIC

Translated by Elżbieta Wójcik-Leese
Introduced by Robert Minhinnick

2013

Published by Arc Publications,
Nanholme Mill, Shaw Wood Road
Todmorden OL14 6DA, UK

Original poems copyright © Krystyna Miłobędzka 2013
Translation copyright © Elżbieta Wójcik-Leese 2013
Introduction copyright © Robert Minhinnick 2013
Copyright in the present edition © Arc Publications 2013

Design & cover photograph by Tony Ward
Printed by Lightning Source

978 1906570 62 0 (pbk)
978 1906570 63 7 (hbk)

ACKNOWLEDGEMENTS

Poems in this collection come from *Zbierane, 1960-2005* (Biuro Literackie, 2006) and *gubione* (Biuro Literackie, 2008). Elżbieta Wójcik-Leese's translations have appeared in the following journals: *Acumen, Brand, Edinburgh Review, Past Simple, Poetry Ireland Review, Poetry Review, Poetry Wales*. The translator acknowledges the support of the Polish Book Institute (SAMPLE TRANSLATIONS grant).

This book is in copyright. Subject to statutory exception and to provision of relevant collective licensing agreements, no reproduction of any part of this book may take place without the written permission of Arc Publications.

Culture

This project has been funded with support from the European Commission. This publication reflects the views only of the author, and the Commission cannot be held responsible for any use which may be made of the information contained therein.

ARTS COUNCIL ENGLAND

Arc Publications 'Visible Poets' series
Series Editor: Jean Boase-Beier

CONTENTS

Series Editor's Note / 9
Translator's Preface / 11
Introduction / 15

22 / "Stawia dwa znaki gwałtowne..." • "It makes two signs, vehement..." / 23
24 / Dom • The house / 25
26 / A przecież zaciśnięte tobie, powtórzone • Quite constricted for you, repeated once again / 27
28 / Pomówimy sobie o byleczym • We'll prattle about any old thing / 29
30 / Wycinanka na dwoje • A cut-out fits two / 31
32 / Jestem że widzę że widzę że mijam • I am that I can see that I can see that I go by / 33
34 / Wycinanka na moje • This cut-out suits me / 35
36 / Tak nas dostało w trzy światy naraz... • So it got us in three worlds simultaneously... / 37
38 / Przesuwanka • Shifting rhyme / 39
40 / Zmówić czego nie wiemy • Pray what we don't know / 41
42 / Imię? • Name? / 43
44 / "staraj się ładnie..." • "try doing it nicely..." / 45
46 / "pomyślę co do dziś..." • "I'll have a think about today..." / 47
48 / "te dwie my stare dziewczynki kobiety..." • "these two us old girls women..." / 49
52 / "nasuwa się łąka..." • "what comes to mind is meadow..." / 53
56 / "tu dom przy domu..." • "here a house beside a house..." / 57
58 / "Boję się twoich coraz większych butów..." • "I am scared of your shoes growing bigger..." / 59
60 / "od kiedy jestem..." • "since the day I became..." / 61
62 / "nawet gdybym zdążyła krzyknąć..." • "even if I managed to quickly shout..." / 63

64 / "patrzę czekam słucham czekam…" • "I look and wait listen and wait…" / 65
64 / "lekko przyszło lekko poszło…" • "easy come easy go…" / 65
66 / "patrzona chodzona żyta…" • "her: looked walked lived…" / 67
68 / "od czego…" • "where do who…" / 69
70 / "w jego śmiechu twoja twarz…" • "in his laughter your face…" / 71
72 / "dziś jest to co mówiłeś będzie…" • "today is what you said would be…" / 73
74 / "nasze teraz pisane dużą literą…" • "our now spelt with a capital letter…" / 75
76 / "przez którą widzi…" • "thanks to her whom he can see…" / 77
78 / "nałożenia…" • "overlaps…" / 79
80 / "z czego zrobić gwiazdę…" • "how to make a star…" / 81
82 / "cisza…" • "silence…" / 83
84 / "Te zapisy…" • "These writings…" / 85
86 / "jest ciszy w pokoju…" • "the is of the silence in the room…" / 87
88 / "może tylko nie ma komu powiedzieć siebie…" • "maybe she has no one to say herself to…" / 89
90 / "moje dziecko…" • "my child…" / 91
90 / "…nieba od ziemi…" • "…heaven from earth…" / 91
92 / "a ja w tym chodzę…" • "and I walk in this…" / 93
92 / "o mnie ze mną?…" • "of me together with me?…" / 93
94 / "obieram kartofle…" • "I peel potatoes…" / 95
96 / "najprędzej gubię czasowniki…" • "I lose verbs quickest…" / 97
98 / "dałem ci ręce…" • "I gave you hands…" / 99
100 / "ich świecenie…" • "their glitter…" / 101
102 / "ciągle ta sama nieopowiadalność!…" • "yet again the same can't-describe!…" / 103
104 / "park mówił sam za siebie…" • "the park spoke for itself…" / 105
106 / "mamy siebie krótko…" • "we have each other briefly…" / 107

108 / "dokładnie czoło…"	"exactly the forehead…" / 109
110 / "kocham cię…"	"I love you…" / 111
112 / "trzy sny…"	"the three dreams…" / 113
114 / "tyle waży…"	"that much weight…" / 115
116 / "wypadł ci pierwszy mleczny ząb…"	"your first milk tooth's just fallen out…" / 117
116 / "…nieba od ziemi…"	"…heaven from earth…" / 117
118 / "przebudzenie…"	"awakening…" / 119
120 / "rozbierz się z Krystyny…"	"strip yourself of Krystyna…" / 121
122 / "jestem do znikania…"	"I am for vanishing…" / 123
124 / "mieszkanie…"	"dwelling…" / 125
126 / "pisz pisz…"	"write write on…" / 127
128 / "w zielono kulisto wysoko ostro…"	"into the green high spherical sharp…" / 129
130 / "jest rosnące drzewem…"	"the is growing into a tree…" / 131
132 / "że jesteś w rozłożystym powietrzu…"	"that you are in the wide branching air…" / 133
132 / "drzewo tak drzewo…"	"the tree yes the tree…" / 133
134 / "próbowałam siebie powiedzieć…"	"I tried to say myself…" / 135
134 / "mówiąc milczę…"	"speaking I'm silent…" / 135
136 / "dróżki w ogrodzie…"	"paths in the garden…" / 137
138 / "ach, to szukanie…"	"ah, this searching…" / 139
138 / "oddziel jasne od słońca…"	"separate bright from the sun…" / 139
140 / "nie pomyśleć nic…"	"not to think nothing…" / 141
140 / "bliżej tych co poszli…"	"closer to those who have gone…" / 141
142 / "w oczy temu…"	"into the eyes…" / 143
144 / "piasek…"	"sand…" / 145
146 / "rzeczowniki…"	"nouns…" / 147
148 / "mów!"	"speak!" / 149
150 / "Jestem…"	"I am…" / 151

Biographical Notes / 152

SERIES EDITOR'S NOTE

The 'Visible Poets' series was established in 2000, and sets out to challenge the view that translated poetry could or should be read without regard to the process of translation it had undergone. Since then, things have moved on. Today there is more translated poetry available and more debate on its nature, its status, and its relation to its original. We know that translated poetry is neither English poetry that has mysteriously arisen from a hidden foreign source, nor is it foreign poetry that has silently rewritten itself in English. We are more aware that translation lies at the heart of all our cultural exchange; without it, we must remain artistically and intellectually insular.

One of the aims of the series was, and still is, to enrich our poetry with the very best work that has appeared elsewhere in the world. And the poetry-reading public is now more aware than it was at the start of this century that translation cannot simply be done by anyone with two languages. The translation of poetry is a creative act, and translated poetry stands or falls on the strength of the poet-translator's art. For this reason 'Visible Poets' publishes only the work of the best translators, and gives each of them space, in a Preface, to talk about the trials and pleasures of their work.

From the start, 'Visible Poets' books have been bilingual. Many readers will not speak the languages of the original poetry but they, too, are invited to compare the look and shape of the English poems with the originals. Those who can are encouraged to read both. Translation and original are presented side-by-side because translations do not displace the originals; they shed new light on them and are in turn themselves illuminated by the presence of their source poems. By drawing the readers' attention to the act of translation itself, it is the aim of these books to make the work of both the original poets and their translators more visible.

Jean Boase-Beier

TRANSLATOR'S PREFACE

Whenever I open a collection of Krystyna Miłobędzka's poetry, the Polish language is coaxed into poems revealing its inner energies. I look, intensely, at and for. The looking becomes hearing; the hearing turns into associating, not only in my readings of the Polish originals, but also in my translations. Miłobędzka shows me that *listen* inhabits the word *glisten*, where I never saw it before. Now, to translate *świecenie*, an important presence in this poetry, I thumb through my English: shine, shimmer, glow, gleam, glitter, glimmer, brightness, radiance, light? Spoilt for choice, I query the poet herself. "I have no idea what the difference is between glitter, light and radiance," replies Miłobędzka, "but to my looking and hearing (and to my, full of dread, associating) I want to avoid radiance (radiation!)."

With Miłobędzka's poems the usual browsing through dictionaries, mental and printed, turns into an etymological – and existential – search. Yet this portmanteau parsing is far from extravagant: her wordings are simple, seemingly ordinary. When I look at the sentence *Lśniło mi się niebo*, I can see the sky, me and the verb which suggests shining. I know that to Miłobędzka verbs are essential, of essence, so I look more closely. This one, reflexive, construes a strange relationship between *the sky* and *me*. What sets out appearing like a simple sentence is heard, oddly, as a slight disturbance, even though the Polish syntax allows its users immense flexibility. Grammatical endings will guide readings, and associations, but in this sentence, suddenly, the sky no longer just shimmers... And Polish readers cannot help but notice that the word *lśniło* contains *śniło*, that is, *dreamt*. "The sky shimmered in my dream" could be my literal translation. But if I experiment and change dreaming to listening? *The sky glistened to me.*

Asked if she considers herself an experimental or avant-garde writer, Miłobędzka admits to difficulties with such labelling. To her, poetry is experimentation, because it tries to

say more in as few words as possible. Moreover, "poetry tries to say that which cannot be said. Therefore, it is ruthless, even cruel, towards language. All poetry which deserves that name leaves its trace on the language we speak."

Experimentation, however ruthless, is an inherent part of writing, and of living. As Miłobędzka explains:

> There comes a moment when you already know certain things, you can hear them, you can do them – that's when you need to run away. You're different in relation to the world: different as a twenty-year-old woman, different after giving birth to your child, different when your child leaves your house. These aren't just roles for you to enter. Rather, that's what you've taken from life and what you return to it. These are reciprocal transactions. You do not settle, you do not fix yourself within the twenty-year-old woman. You experience things and these experiences change you, and they change your writing, if you happen to write at the time.

Miłobędzka, born in 1932, first published in 1960; ever since, within her twelve poetry collections, she has demonstrated her unwillingness to settle for the fixed solutions language offers so readily. She knows that what you happen to write down can never match what you want to write about: "Words are always late." Or, as she put it in one of her poems:

> These writings. Well, that's what they are, not what I'd like them to be. All the time weaker than that which exists. They drag on for years, fail to keep pace.

Keeping pace with what there *is* – another important Miłobędzka verb, not at all weak or invisible or immobile; the verb that embodies the multiplicity of being and beings – requires movement (being on the move), speed and selection. So you resort to shorthand, "the poetics of jottings", as the poet describes her writing. To quickly signal one being, one thought, before – while – you see, hear, smell, taste, touch, think another. Where words are stepping stones for readers jumping from one experience to another down the Heraclitean brook. Down, not across, because this passage is

not about the crossing, but about the flow.

Language itself is on the move, so the stepping stones turn out to be slippery pebbles or wobbly chunks of rock. Miłobędzka herself chips off her phrases, makes them unstable, selects shorter, smaller words, "words broken in half broken to quarters". She chooses prepositions as her favoured part of speech: "There's nothing more important, more tender and mysterious than prepositions. It isn't nouns and verbs that set the world (text) in motion, but prepositions. Prepositions cause children a lot of speaking difficulties, with their multiple functions, instability, lack of fixed position in a sentence." However, the Polish sentence has grammatical means to steer listeners and readers in the right direction, when its flow is deliberately disturbed to allow skirting or gliding, to cause whirls and eddies.

How to convey this verbal sketchiness, phrasal instability, syntactic re-shuffle in English? Risking a slower pace, at times I impose visual boundaries, insert blanks, change the lineation of the original prose poem. I experiment, though I have stopped short of imitating Emily Dickinson, listed by Miłobędzka together with Bolesław Leśmian, Miron Białoszewski, Tymoteusz Karpowicz (three Polish poets hardly known in English translation) as the four experimenters she reads carefully. Among her prose favourites she counts the writings of Bruno Schulz and Leopold Buczkowski, as well as *Alice in Wonderland*.

Besides jotting words and whittling phrases to their particles, another Miłobędzka strategy to "perform this moment in words" is *not* writing. Hers is also the poetics of crossings-out.

> to cross out every (second) thought (word)
> from the remaining (every) third to write down
> and then...
> and then...   ... ...

One of *twelve poems in colour* (published in 2012, though written – or crossed-out? – in 2009) continues with the sign of the ellipsis for five more lines. To my relief as its translator?

Not quite, because Miłobędzka expects co-effort from me as her reader: "Not saying something in a text is the very place which, I believe, readers will enter with their own thinking." This necessity to cross things out derives also from Miłobędzka's growing awareness that writing something down is less and less necessary.

My selected translations end with poems from *After a Shout* (2004) and *one by one lost* (2008) – two volumes of jottings which testify to Miłobędzka's conviction that "we are destined to disappear". Not as a surrender or failure, but rather – in Beckett's wording – in order to *leasten*. "For then in utmost dim to unutter leastmost all", as the speaker of *Worstward Ho* explains. 'Unuttering' and 'leastening' do not suggest 'silencing'. Against the grains of ellipses and sand, Miłobędzka prompts: *mów!*, even though she is aware of the shortcomings of human speech. "Speak, say on…", as her translator I try out alternatives, contemplating Beckett's monosyllables: "On. Stare on. Say on. Be on. Somehow on." They may well have urged my English versions.

I have stayed on with these poems, because they "simultaneously close and open a world" (as Miłobędzka commented on Basho, another presence important to her), the way you close and open a house. "Try building a house from words", writes Miłobędzka in a poem which considers both the necessity and futility of such an exercise. But it is not a mere exercise. Miłobędzka has studied children's theatre and written plays for children, so she understands the dramatic, and poetic, potential of this activity, this act: "The world comes to being in early childhood and, thinking or speaking about the house, I always find there myself and that which I cannot name."

Like stones, words can be used for building a house: be they Polish words, English words, old words, new words – words we have experimented with. In that house we may find ourselves and that which we cannot name.

Elżbieta Wójcik-Leese

INTRODUCTION

Frankly, translation puzzles me. There is so much writing in the world, who has time for translation except the practitioners? Isn't it secondary art because essentially reductive? That question arises from how we seem to define 'translation' itself. As if it was copying one language into another, rather like what occurs in the bureaucratic hives of the European Community, when exactitudes are demanded.

Of course, translation means something other in a largely monolingual UK than it does in multilingual cultures. (I write this in Wales, officially, though raggedly, one of the few 'bilingual' parts of that UK. Eighty percent of people in Wales, out of three million, simply ignore the Welsh they see around them, or learn how not to see it – there is a word for this behaviour – or spend their lives in bafflement.)

However, what excites me, when I translate, is musical possibility. Translation can provide the chance to remix, rescore, or yes, rewrite someone else's writing, if that writing sufficiently intrigues, fascinates, inspires, challenges. The translator should feel enabled to use a different tempo or time signature, even a different key, from the original music. To leave out, or add, 'notes' or 'staves'. To ensure the writing works in the new language. In all, to make *differently*. To *recreate*. Even deconstruct. But not unmake. And never *uncreate*.

Yes, what I seek in poetry, increasingly, is music. The barest, most minimal music it might be, yet music all the same. Perhaps I am still recovering after editing a poetry magazine for eleven years, an experience that taught me after reading countless thousands of submissions (mainly from British, Irish, North American, and Australian people) that most of us who write poems do not imagine the musical possibilities of language.

If poetry is a musical art, at least an art with immense

musical possibilities, then how a poem sounds should be as important as its meaning. But the quest for 'meaning' means the death of poetry. The question of what a poem 'means' has marginalised criticism and perverted reading. It has delivered a death sentence to the curiosity of many people who have become alienated from 'poetry'.

Writers are often asked "what do you write about?". It's difficult to respond "very little". But answering "I write about the sound of sand blowing against the glass of an amusement arcade" begs too many futile questions. Yet writers are never asked about how their writing *sounds*. (Are composers asked what they write about? Are songwriters?) If poetry concerns music, my answer to the question is no, translation is not a secondary art.

2

I first encountered Elżbieta Wójcik-Leese's translations from the Polish when I edited the quarterly *Poetry Wales*. I was immediately happy to publish. Those poems were clear and yet possessed of an enigmatic quality that demanded rereading. Above all, they were excellent poems in themselves, that is, poems in English. The translator was indisputably a poet. As I understood no Polish, my only demand was that Wójcik-Leese's poems were successful in this 'translated' language. Were they 'faithful' to the originals? Did the Polish poets approve? I didn't inquire.

At the same time I was publishing poetry 'translated' from all over the world. Such is life as a literary editor of an English language magazine. But Wójcik-Leese immediately seemed the real thing. She had chosen her poems for a reason. In a way, they had become her property, as she had devoted herself intimately to their new existence in English.

The poems in *Nothing More* are chosen from almost the whole of Krystyna Miłobędzka's writing life. The first poem is from her debut collection, published when she was twenty-eight, the latter half of *Nothing More* from later volumes, some poems dating from her seventies. Given a

choice, it is the older poet I would seek out, her later poems written after a real life lived. They are authoritative and devastating in their honesty.

> Strip yourself of Krystyna
> of child mother woman
> lodger lover tourist wife
>
> What's left is undressing
> trails of discarded clothes
> light gestures, nothing more.

And in the next poem simply:

> I am for vanishing.

The language is stark. Not that it was ever ornate. But these later poems are impelled by realisation that life becomes more interesting when we divest ourselves of our comforts. When we rid ourselves of certainties. Only then is the true self revealed. Otherwise, life is hidden. Or camouflaged by the superfluous. Ultimately, we must vanish. Only by 'vanishing' are we released and is pretence abandoned.

Increasingly I agree with this, although I am still addicted to the superfluities, suspecting that if ever successful in finding our 'true essence' then that will prove disappointing. Yet how wonderful Krystyna Miłobędzka makes *vanishing* seem. But first we must disappear from ourselves, only then to others. Because we all vanish, atom by atom, until we are unrecognisable to our former selves.

I like the progress of *Nothing More*. We see how Miłobędzka learns people do not, and cannot, remain the same. What she was when a girl she could and can be no longer. (But were we ever really as we recall?) Always the *then* informs the *now*. Makes it inescapable. And yet the *'isness'* of the present is not the *'wasness'* of the past.

There's an understanding of the almost Alzheimic quality to life – "I lose verbs quickest" – because language is something else that vanishes, is put aside, although not necessarily at rates of our own choosing. Language itself ablates, thaws like frost, or retreats like a glacier, leaving

incomprehensible debris stranded in awkward places.

There is real fear in this, because no, the poet is not always impossibly fatalistic:

> not to think nothing
> dread to think nothing

And there is wisdom in Miłobędzka, but it is not inexplicable. This poet's wisdom is demanding but not daunting.

In addition to my poetry, it's my attempts to write English fiction that have helped me appreciate *Nothing More*. As I become older I realise memory is not seamless but irregular and erratic. Many things are forgotten, but so much that is unimportant is recalled. And what, I increasingly wonder, divides memory from dreams? And what from imagination? From fantasy? What we actually remember is always changing. Because memory is organic and volatile. Memory is molten. So how are memories to be trusted as they ghost in and out of the mind?

Yes, in a way a memory is like a translated poem. And a poem, of course, can never be 'translated' because its actuality cannot be transferred into a new language. All translations of poems are 'versions' or 're-creations'. Nor can there be 'definitive' translation. If poetry is a musical art, every 'version' and 'recreation' is valid. Which does not guarantee that they are any good.

Miłobędzka implies that we should see our lives as attics. Or spare rooms. Or sheds. Or writers' notebooks. Full of what we no longer need, accumulations once important and necessary, now irrelevant.

Then, in the end is... what? Sand, it seems. Everything is sand, or sand is everywhere? And Miłobędzka is not unironic about the business of writing: "when in need every word turns into a trophy." Such deadly accuracy.

Initially, Miłobędzka was not prolific. The first collection appeared in 1960, succeeded by volumes in 1970, 1975, 1984. Publications have become more frequent in later years, but the poems are shorter. (Or the surrounding pages larger?)

The last poem in *Nothing More* seems a cod bio. An unexpected satirical flourish? Its target is those self-written biographies that writers are compelled to publish, listing awards and defining their place in the *litbiz* pecking order. This poem could be a subversion of what contemporary 'poetry' has come to mean: 'celebrity poets', poetry 'readings', poetry 'festivals', poetry 'tours', websites. The whole sickening gallimaufry. Such biographies are present in this book. Because that's the way we do things. Now.

I'm not sure how Miłobędzka would answer if someone inquired what her poetry means. Or how it sounds. I'm not even certain whether in later life she writes 'individual poems', possibly preferring to think of all her writing as 'jotting'. But her advice on writing is advice about life. Here are quotations from throughout this book:

> write write on till you vanish in writing
> look look on till you vanish in looking
>
> strip yourself of Krystyna
>
> what's left is undressing
>
> when in need every word turns into a trophy
>
> we have each other for eternal wonder
>
> does it feel green to be grass

Her writing now has crystallized into a series of aphorisms. But Miłobędzka is also a mother musing on her own identity. She senses herself dissolving as her child becomes increasingly vivid:

> I am scared of your shoes growing bigger...
>
> I wanted to hold on to your little birth
>
> the whole screaming life suddenly in my hands

Disappearing in this way is more interesting than reading of someone accruing 'stuff'. Isn't the writer challenging us to divest ourselves of certainty? How we vanish is as

important as how we emerge.

The later writing in *Nothing More* seems irreducible. It is so acute as to be difficult to single out quotations. But one ominous note is sounded:

> kneel down
> turn back
>
> silence
> no word for the woods in snow

Miłobędzka was, of course, a child between the world wars. That experience must permeate her life.

As the poems become shorter, so the poet confronts the impossibility of expressing what she needs to convey: the '*is*ness' of being, the timelessness of the present moment. And:

> We'll prattle about any old thing.

Yes, poets will. People do.

Writing can concern creating an identity, and also understanding that identity is temporary. By the time we've learned who we are we've already changed. And are changing. Each of us is a work in progress. People 'emerge' then gradually 'disappear'.

Finally, Miłobędzka is writing about inescapable domestic routines, realising work is prayer and prayer is life. That poetry too is prayer. Occasionally it scintillates:

> gentian
> the invincible sapphire of this word

And, thanks to her translator, bursts into surprising flower:

> childishly green short breathless winter wheat

Wójcik-Leese is not remixing or rewriting Miłobędzka. She is attempting something braver and far more subtle. I view the poems in *Nothing More* as collaborations. They are the fruits of an exemplary literary symbiosis.

Robert Minhinnick

NOTHING MORE

Stawia dwa znaki gwałtowne, wzniesione do pędu, próbuje pusty rozmach koła, z góry strzęp lotu, znak ostrzem zadany niecelnie, rozparte furkoce w potrzasku, podrywa z uporem, wpada w miękką obręcz bez znaku nadziei. Słucham „pióro" i patrzę „pióro". Mówię ściśnięte, wybiega ku górze puszyście, opada z lękiem, wije się w gniazdo.

It makes two signs, vehement, ready for the uprush, attempts an empty sweep of a circle, a scrap of a swoop, a miscalculated stab; sprawled, it flutters in its trap, stubbornly springs off the ground, falls into a soft hoop, hopeless. I can hear 'pióro', and I can see 'pióro' and 'quill'. I utter this constriction: feathery, it runs upward, then drops in fright, weaves itself into a nest.

DOM

Trzyma mnie w swoim wnętrzu, nisko od korzeni do ciemności drzewa mój cień jego ruchem cieniem, a pory roku pędzą w gęstwinę. Dotykam pierwszych ścian przez grubość lat, przez życia ubiegłe do kory, między kołyską i drzwiami w twarde drewno wryty przypływ. Ze skraju, z drgnienia ma wejście jedyne: wysoko po skórze drze płomień do szumu w kołowrót zieleni, aż skrzypią ramiona. Gdzie dotknie polany, wyrębu w pamięci?

THE HOUSE

holds me in its interior low from the roots to the darkness
of the tree my shadow becomes its movement its shadow
and the seasons rush headlong into the thicket.
I touch its first walls through the thickness
of years through lives gone into the bark between cradle
and doors the tide cut deeply into hard wood.
From the edge from the quiver it has one entrance only:
high up the flame tears along the skin towards the whirr
in the windlass of green until the arms creak.
Where will it touch the meadow the clearing in memory?

A PRZECIEŻ ZACIŚNIĘTE TOBIE, POWTÓRZONE

Ciemno mi nad tym, gołąbku, co prędko uderza. Teraz jeszcze we mnie trzepocesz na syna na ojca, mało ci słychu widu śluzu, mało ciekawie. Podobno krzyk usłyszymy. Czekamy, spodziewamy się mało ciekawie.

QUITE CONSTRICTED FOR YOU, REPEATED ONCE AGAIN

So dark, my little bird, over what's beating
fast inside me now. Still in me you are
fluttering: of the son, and of the father.
Still not that much for you to listen to,
not enough mucus or view,
hardly a thrill. Apparently we will hear
a scream. We've been waiting,
expecting hardly a thrill.

POMÓWIMY SOBIE O BYLECZYM

Wydobycie głowy z worka, trud tego szamotania, przerwy jakby się nie powiodło umarło. Ruchy konwulsyjne i odpoczywanie w dziwacznych pozach. Wciąganie ręki czy głowy już wydobytej, nowe skoki wewnątrz worka. „Urodzona" ręka chwyta powietrze, potem leżącego obok – „nagie" w gnieździe, zwinięte w „jajo". Prostowanie ramion, próby lotu kończące się upadkiem i powrotem do gniazda – relacja z tego. Dmuchanie w pióro rzucone w powietrze. Pióro spada. Brak tchu, łapanie pióra, żeby za nim wzlecieć – relacja z tego. Oglądanie olbrzymich piór i kolorowych wstążek, próba ze wstążką – nawijanie, szukanie jej początku (końca), ciągnięcie (upadek). Ptak chce wzlecieć, człowiek go ogranicza. Łączenie piór i wstążek, przywiązywanie piór wstążkami do rąk do głów – relacja z tego. Wiązanie się wstążką jak na wspinaczce.

Sticking its head out of the bag, the struggle of this scuffle, the pauses as if it all aborted died. Convulsive movements and moments of rest in awkward poses. Tucking in the hand or the head that's already been out, new jumps inside the bag. The 'born' hand grasps first the air then the one lying beside – the 'naked' in the nest, curled up, an 'egg'. The stretching of the arms, attempted flights which end in falls and returns to the nest – reporting this. Blowing into a feather thrown up in the air. The feather drops. Out of breath, chasing the feather to soar after it – reporting this. Watching enormous feathers and multi-coloured ribbons, rehearsing with a ribbon – winding it round, looking for its beginning (its end), pulling it (its fall). The bird wants to fly up, the man limits this flight. Tying ribbons and feathers, fastening feathers with ribbons to the hands to the heads – reporting this. Securing oneself with a ribbon as if during a climb.

WYCINANKA NA DWOJE

ja dopasowana, w twoich oczach

rozszerzona, przeniesiona śmiesznie

strasznie

i nawzajem

oślepieni sobą we mnie, tak się mamy z oczu w rękach

zachwyceni

A CUT-OUT FITS TWO

me well-matched, in your eyes

widened, projected awkwardly

horribly

and mutually

blinded in me, we own each other from sight to touch

enraptured

JESTEM ŻE WIDZĘ ŻE WIDZĘ ŻE MIJAM

późno mi, jeszcze musi nas wystarczyć razem

głos ruch widzę prześwituję, patrzysz przeze mnie i poprzez, tam też nie tak gęsto a gęsto od ludzi

coraz mniej ja

tyle schowana przed tobą między zwierzęta, co drugie co trzecie przybiega do mnie, wtedy jestem żywa

nie mam innego sposobu prócz zabrać by oddać

I AM THAT I CAN SEE THAT I CAN SEE THAT I GO BY

I feel late, together we shall last a little longer

voice movement that I can see that I am see-through, you look through me and throughout, there are no crowds yet crowds of people

less and less of me

that much of me hidden from you among the animals, every second every third runs up to me, then I am alive

I have no other means but to take in order to give back

WYCINANKA NA MOJE

Słyszysz mi się duży schowany, z miesiąca na księżyc okrąglejesz – może ja? I jeszcze jedno, bliższe ucho – może ja? kiedy moje? Siadam idę, na widoczne na jadalne

a ty śpij, bo warto

dopóki ja ci tego, tylko nie płacz, tego nie przegryzę.

THIS CUT-OUT SUITS ME

You   I can hear you, hidden and big   month after moon growing fuller – or is it me? One more, closer, ear – could it be me? when mine? I sit and walk   what's visible what's edible

go to sleep now, it will do you good

until I, don't you cry, until I bite it in two.

TAK NAS DOSTAŁO W TRZY ŚWIATY NARAZ NIEDOKŁADNIE NASZE A KAŻDY RODZINNY (KOŁYSANKA)

to tak – i w ledwo tobie ledwo z nas

patrzę słyszę

wrona już ci ze mnie idzie, za mnie tobie po górce chodzi

czy dojdzie i na drzewo które głośniej przyznasz

stamtąd tu i dokąd (raz pierze, raz deska)

czy w bucikach, czy dojdę, dojdziemy coś jeszcze, gdzie światami huczy

w imię ojca mnie i syna

to tak ciężko i ładnie trafić w między nami pytające

SO IT GOT US IN THREE WORLDS SIMULTANEOUSLY INACCURATELY OURS AND EACH FAMILIAL (A LULLABY)

so this is it – in barely you barely out of us

I look and I can hear

a crow of me is walking up to you, instead of me
it's walking up the hill

will it reach the peak, the tree you'll approve more noisily

from there up to here, where to? (once feathers, once planks)

in these tiny shoes, will I make it, will we reach something else, where the wild worlds roar

in the name of the father myself and the son

it's so hard and pretty to hit upon our in-between questioning

PRZESUWANKA

stąd tu

tu, nie tam

tam, gdzie jest

jest, gdzie był

był, gdzie będzie bo

wszędzie dobrze, gdzie nas nie ma

nie ma nas tam

tam, nie tu!

tu, gdzie jesteśmy

jesteśmy, gdzieśmy byli

będziemy, gdzie byliśmy, synku – od ciebie chciałam zacząć nowymi słowami, ale nie umiem

SHIFTING RHYME

to here

here, not there

there where he is

is where he was

was where he will be because

everywhere's fine wherever we are not

no, we are not there

there, not here!

here where we are

we are where we were

we will be where we were, son – from you on I was supposed to start with new words, but I don't know how

ZMÓWIĆ CZEGO NIE WIEMY

Nie mogę ruszyć się z domu. Moje plecy są czwartą ścianą, moja noga zastępuje drzwi. Kiedy odejdę, dom runie. Jeżeli wstanę i pójdę do ciebie, nie będę miała domu.

Nasłuchuję, wypatruję oczy. Wypada na jeszcze. Światy światy tego, a tu same streszczenia. „Jeszcze" na luzie ugania. Ze spodziewania w zapomnienie, skurczona na ziemi czy łóżku we wnuczkę prababkę i głębiej. Tymczasem. Na potem.

O potem, potem! Będziesz światłem, głosem, wieżą.

PRAY WHAT WE DO NOT KNOW

I can't move from the house. My back is its fourth wall, my leg replaces its door. When I leave, the house will collapse. If I get up, if I come to you, I will lose my home.

I'm all ears, I'm straining my eyes. There's more yet to come. Worlds and worlds of it, but here merely summaries. 'Yet' on the loose. From expectation into forgetting, shrunk on the ground or on the bed curled into granddaughter great-grandmother deeper still. Meanwhile. For later.

O later, later! You'll become light, a voice, a tower.

IMIĘ?

to za mamę, to za tatę, to za pieska, to za myszkę. Po łyżeczce, po łyżeczce, po łyżeczce. Temu dała na listeczku, temu dała w garnuszeczku, temu dała na talerzyczku, temu

nic nie zostało. Ja pudełko puste, błysk wieczka.

KTOTOTAKI?   NIEOTOCHODZI

NAME?

one for mummy, one for daddy, one for doggy, one for mousey. One spoonful, another spoonful, and another spoonful. On a little leaf, in a little cup, on a little plate – for the one

nothing more left. Me an empty box, a flicker of the lid.

WHOSTHAT?   THATSNOTTHEPOINT

staraj się ładnie równo pokolorować te puste białe ręce nogi twarze

to są czarne drzewa w zimie, to niebo wieczorem, twoja matka to są stare suknie, słowa w pół ćwierć przerwane

rano rodzenie ścielenie, odsłanianie mimo wszystko, i parę własnych kroków dalej, na resztę nie miałam, mimo wszystko zabrakło mi, nie wyszłam przez te kilkadziesiąt lat z wielkiego koła światła, dręcząca jasność powtarzania, przypomnij sobie

roześmiana dziewczynka trzyma w rękach blaszaną puszkę na której roześmiana dziewczynka trzyma w rękach puszkę z roześmianą dziewczynką która trzyma dziewczynkę głębej na wierzchu puszki w rękach coraz mniejszej puszki puszkę dziewczynkę

znam siebie najlepiej z widzenia i słyszenia innych, uczyłam się powtarzać, powtarzanie sprawiało mi wielką trudność, wciąż źle wymawiam długie schody i szybkie bicie serca, nie mówiłam śniegu, nie miałam tak czystej sposobności

dokoła się kręci płacz na śmiech zachodzi obiad na dziś jest jutro a jeszcze wczoraj nie mam, nie znalazłam

try doing it nicely evenly colour in these empty white hands legs faces

these are black trees in winter this is an evening sky your mother these are old dresses words broken in half broken to quarters

morning birth-giving bed-making uncovering despite all and a few of my own steps further I hadn't enough for the rest despite all I ran out all those years unable to cross the enormous circle of light the nagging lucidity of repetition bear it in mind

a laughing girl holds a tin can where a laughing girl holds a can with a laughing girl who holds a girl deeper on the surface of the can in the hands of the smaller and smaller can the can and the girl

I know myself best by the eye and the ear of others I learnt how to repeat repeating was very difficult I still mispronounce long stairwells and quick heartbeat I haven't uttered snow yet no such pure opportunity

round and round it circles tears and laughter overlap dinner for today is tomorrow but I haven't got yesterday haven't found it yet

pomyślę co do dziś ani jutro też z głową w praniu po łokcie
po czym nogami boże boże ile ty znowu naniosłeś piachu
po kostki do obiadu mam jeszcze całe szycie w dziurach
na kolanach od okna do drzwi za każdym dzwonkiem
dziecko gdzie ty biegasz odetchnij odetnij literkę od literki
te się znowu składa w co zechcesz napiszę:

I'll have a think about today not even tomorrow with my head in the washing up to my elbows then again with the legs my goodness look how much sand you've brought home up to the ankles till it's time for dinner I have all the sewing full of holes on the knees from window to door with each doorbell son where are you off to now take it easy take it apart one letter cut from another letter then again assembled in whatever you want I will write:

te dwie my stare dziewczynki kobiety

o czym mówimy sobie? O huśtaniu dziecka od lalki do lalki „lalka po niej". Rodzina słów. Mówią „powtórz", co ona próbuje powtórzyć dziecku. Ta moja lekka pewność ciebie „dziecino". Gdzie ja cię z przepaści wyniosę, gdzie po cieniutku ukryję? Czy coś jeszcze tak mocno obdarzę życiem? Krążenie nad nami, tupanie

nasze nieutulone czepia się sprzętów, sprzątań. Rodzina stołów, rodzina drzwi. To jest mężczyzna wybrany na życie spośród niewielu znajomych „ty mi tym nie świeć w oczy". Jedno ma w boku ranę na drugie, każde w swoim własnym niewyobrażeniu na obraz o drugim „widzę że mnie nie widzisz, ja ci tym w oczy nie świecę". W coś razem żyjemy, wmawiamy się sobie. Rodzina ścian, rodzina głosów. Na to niepewne, niewiadome gdzie teraz. Obrus w zielone koniczynki, czerwone serca, przetarty od składania na pół, na ćwierć. Ty wydobędziesz go dla. Ty wydobędziesz go dla. Blisko oddalona krzyczy szeptem

z nie wiem, z nie rozumiem, ze strachu przed nie wiem, nie rozumiem, co to ona mówi? „Tak żeby skapywało z łyżki" dała przepis na wypiek tani i wypróbowany. „Co z ciebie mam? jeden strach więcej." „Mama czy te świeczki to są świeczki czy lata?" Rodzina głosów, rodzina ech. W otoczeniu bliskich bliska, a obcujemy obcy i to bez związku w coś się wiąże. A kiedyś, kiedy mi się otworzą oczy. Była cała wszyta w obrąbek od pieluszki do ostatniego prześcieradła, tajemnica jej przeszyć dla mnie, pytanie o igłę

these two us old girls women

what are we chatting about? About rocking a child from doll to doll, 'a hand-me-down doll'. A family of words. They say 'repeat', which she tries to repeat to her child. My weightless confidence in you 'kid'. Where will I carry you out of this chasm, where will I shelter you narrowly? Will I gift life to anything else with equal strength? The circling above us, the stomping

our unsoothed clings to the objects, orderliness. A family of tables, a family of doors. This is the man chosen for life from scarce acquaintances, 'don't you shine this straight into my eyes'. One has a wounded side for the other, each in their own inconceivableness in the image of the other. 'I can see you no longer see me, I don't shine this straight into your eyes'. Together we live a make-believe, we talk ourselves into each other's heads. A family of walls, a family of voices. On this not certain, not known where to now. The tablecloth green clovers, red hearts, worn out from frequent folding in half, in quarter. You will fetch it for. You will fetch it for. Closely distant she shouts in whisper

out of I don't know, out of I don't get it, fearing the I don't know, I don't get it, what is she saying? 'So that it drips off the spoon' she gave me this cheap fool-proof recipe. 'What's the use of you? One fear more.' 'Mum, are these candles candles or years?' A family of voices, a family of echoes. Surrounded by close relatives, I'm close; strangers, we mix with other strangers and what's unrelated somehow starts to relate. One day, when my eyes open wide. She was all sewn into the hem from the terry nappy to the last sheet, the secret of her sewing transformations, questions about a needle

co to nam mówi? „przebiję, przebyję." Te dwie, my, stare małe dziewczynki, zakrzątane słowa, co to mówi? O huśtaniu dziecka od lalki do lalki (lalka po niej) „teraz jest całe jak dawniej, jak nowe" „nie krusz i tak są plamy". Nasze nieutulone czepia się ścian stołów serwet, jakby mogło

jak gdyby one mogły, czy są dość jasne gdyby

dość wysokie, czy nas jasno i wysoko podrzucą, wytłumaczą?

what does it tell us? 'I will pierce it, I'll traverse it.' These two, us, old little girls, busy-bodied words, what does it say? About rocking a child from doll to doll (a hand-me-down doll), 'it's as good as new now' 'mind the crumbs, it's all stains'. Our unsoothed clings to the walls tables doilies, as if it could

as if they could, are they bright enough if

tall enough, will we be thrown bright and high in the air, will we be clarified?

nasuwa się łąka, łąka łąk ta jedna na starość

przywykam do mijania twarzy

grobek w piasku, kwiatki krzyżyk „muszę zobaczyć kto tam czy mewa ryba nic", za falę będzie po nim

morza mam tyle ile przy nim stoję, nie pilnowane rozpływa się w szare nie wiem

to taki sam leśny różowy goździk „takich już nie będzie" mówił ojciec

mucha chodzi po ręce

leżę i jest tak równo że prócz pojedynczych słów na rzeczy obok mnie nic się nie zdarza

róża – chwilę myślę o kolcach wbitych w rękę, to moje żywe otwarcie na inne, dlaczego tylko ten krótki mały ból łączy mnie z czymkolwiek?

chciałabym żeby bolało mnie wszystko dokoła ale ono jest i jest i czeka

czy powiedzenie ciebie to duża rzecz? większa niż ty większa od wszystkiego mniejszej?

nie mów świat dopóki nie przeskoczysz

what comes to mind is meadow   the meadow of meadows the one for my old age

slowly I'm getting used to the passage of faces

a small grave in the sand   a small cross and some flowers 'I need to see who it is, seagull fish nothing'   in a wave it'll be gone

sea   that much of it as I stand on its shore   unattended it spills slurs into the grey I don't know

that's the same pink forest carnation   'soon none of these will be left', my father used to say

a fly walking on my arm

I'm lying   it's so flat that apart from a few single words to name things beside me nothing happens

a rose – briefly I think of its thorns piercing my hand that's my live opening onto the other   why only such a short slight pain can connect me to anything out there?

I wish what's around me would hurt me but instead it exists and exists and waits

is uttering you a big thing? bigger than you bigger than everything than   smaller?

don't count the world before it is hatched

szkoda mi tych niskich chmur, coraz ich mniej do zobaczenia

z ojcem też takie widzenia przez sen przez fotografię

widzenia, słyszenia, dotknięcia

what a pity these low clouds are so rarely seen

same with my father similar sightings in photographs in dreams

sightings   hearings   touches

tu dom przy domu bez „tu dom"

tu co łączy po łączy tu wie że biegnie do „za późno" i biegnie

myśli o tej myśli

gdziekolwiek ta rzecz ten przedmiot ja siebie traci zaczyna

chciałaby o tu sobie ale gdzie ja się od dzieli od ty

chciałaby tu coś mieć swojego i zaraz krzyczeć to drobić to matka z pustymi rękami tu niosła tu śpiewała tu ją śniło

umarli głaszczą mnie po głowie oni się już nie wstydzą czułości

śni mi się że żyję z równym trudem przychodzi nam podłoga mowa wyciągnięcie ręki

po coś śnię że jestem

z ojca matki nijaka z dnia nocy szara to jej nie wyjdzie na zdrowie na złe na dobre na nie

idzie po co patrzy na drzewa czy im doda zieleni

tu wielka góra teraz i zawsze mam iść spaść iść wisieć iść słyszeć iść krzyczeć dosyć iść?

zanim odemknie usta oczy całe się rozpadnie ja osobno boli osobno płacz osobno się

here a house beside a house without 'here is a house'

here what connects will re connect here it knows that it runs up to 'too late' and runs on

thoughts about this thought

wherever this thing this object I loses itself begins

she'd love just here herself but where will the I dis connect from you

she'd love to have something of her own here and soon to shout it out to chop it up empty-handed mother here she carried here she sang here she was dreamt about

the dead stroke me on my head no longer shying from tenderness

I dream that I live with equal difficulty a floor speech an extended hand occur to us

there must be a reason why I dream that I am

of the father of the mother featureless of day and night grey this will do her no good no wrong no

she goes but why does she look at the trees will she add to their greenness

here a high mountain now and forever I have to go fall go hang go hear go shout enough go?

before she opens her mouth her eyes the whole will disperse the whole I separate in pain separate in tears separate itself

Boję się twoich coraz większych butów. Te okna pytania coraz większe, kiedy biegniesz ulicą.

Ja tu wciąż jestem. We wciąż drobniejszym, ciaśniejszym, co zostaje ze starego snu.

W deszczu, w brudnym świetle dnia tego deszczu. Chciałam się chwycić twego małego urodzenia.

Życie moje dziecko. Całe krzyczące życie nagle w moich rękach. Nie jestem tak silna.

(One takie są, one wszystkie. Wypuszczają dzieci przed siebie. Nie żeby trafiły. Żeby biegły.)

I am scared of your shoes growing bigger. All these windows these questions growing bigger while you're running down the street.

I am still here. In the still which gets ever so small, cramped, a remnant of some old dream.

In the rain, in the dirty light of the day of that rain. I wanted to hold on to your little birth.

Life my child. The whole screaming life suddenly in my hands. I haven't got that much strength.

(They are like that, all of them. They let their children go ahead. Not to find their way. To run.)

od kiedy jestem

cząstką domu

cząstką dziecka

cząstką jednego nieskończonego zdania, cząstka to moje największe imię

cząstką śmierci cząstką życia, przyzwyczajenia powtórzenia łzy w samą porę, tej sukni coraz więcej na mnie

cały ojciec, kto te wianuszki haftował

tamte jaśniutkie włosy

cząstką śmierci (śmierć cząstką życia) dobrze że go tak zawsze mamy przed oczami, córki w duże lekkie kwiaty, teraz już same lekkie kwiaty, zabierz mnie stąd

since the day I became

part of the house

part of the child

part of this one unfinished sentence, the part has grown to be my biggest name

part of death part of life   routines repetitions tears just in time   this dress larger and larger on me

just like the father   and who has embroidered these little wreaths?

that fine fair hair

part of death (death as part of life) it's good to always have him before our eyes   the daughters in big weightless flowers   now only the big weightless flowers left   take me away from here

nawet gdybym zdążyła krzyknąć jestem tej najniższej
chmurze, jesteś będzie już inne, w innym miejscu

even if I managed to quickly shout I am to this lowest cloud,
you are will be already different, in a different place

patrzę czekam słucham czekam
idę czekam jem czekam śpię czekam

ani dnia ani godziny

ani siebie ani ciebie
ani stąd ani dotąd

gdzie się to dzieje podziało

                                                lekko przyszło lekko poszło
                                                nie zostawiło śladu

                                                z blasku w blask
                                                z otwartego w otwarte

                                                nie płakało nie śmiało się
                                                nie miało twarzy

I look and wait listen and wait
walk and wait eat wait sleep wait

neither the day nor the hour

neither myself nor you
neither from here nor up to there

where's this going on   gone

                                        easy come easy go
                                        leaving not a trace

                                        from brightness into
                                        brightness

                                        from the open
                                        into the open

                                        didn't cry didn't laugh
                                        didn't have a face

patrzona chodzona żyta
byta
płakana mówiona

jej jest i jej będzie
jej pisane i jej niepisane

te cości i nicości

her: looked walked lived
been
shed in tears uttered in words

her is and her will-be
her written and her unwritten

these things and nothings

od czego
od kogo, zanim zacznę

który pierwszy, który mój, który naj
i którą ci siebie na zawsze zostawię
dlaczego tę w śmiechu z warkoczami zdyszaną
którą zostawię ci siebie z której głębokiej szuflady
na której fotografii odbitej nieostro
tę o ciebie starszą, tę o tobie cichą
tę w ostatniej chwili dobiegłą

twarz wśród twarzy, w jasnej smudze poruszona
z wysoko uniesionymi brwiami
to zdziwienie wszędzie nie na miejscu
na brzegu morza, na skraju lasu, na brzeżku łóżka
na końcu języka

where do who
do I before I begin

who first, who mine, who best
which of my selves shall I leave you for good
why the one laughing with plaits out of breath
which of my selves shall I leave you from which deep drawer
in which photograph developed but blurred
the one older by you, the one silent about you
the one at the last minute running up to here

a face among faces, moved in a bright streak
with the eyebrows raised high
this astonishment everywhere out of place
on the shore of the sea, verge of the woods, edge of the bed
tip of the tongue

w jego śmiechu twoja twarz dokładna i bliska
rozlega się echem, wraca mniejsza: wnuk ci się zaśmiał ojcze

nie mogę stracić cię z oczu, tracę
chcę mówić o tobie, siebie słyszę

nie droga, nie ścieżka
węziej wyżej
poprzez coś co zaraz po tobie
po wstaje po wraca
do przed chwilą trąconej sandałem gałązki

tylko na ociupinę
na parę okrągłych złoceń przy literach

tam w górze nasza ścieżka
tam w dole nasza ścieżka
idziemy razem przez wielki porządek gór
niżej połupane kamienie
najniżej kwiaty

gencjana
niepokonany szafir tego słowa

biegniemy szybką kroplą po ciemnym liściu

in his laughter your face, precise and near,
echoes and returns smaller: your grandson laughed, father

I cannot lose sight of you   I lose it
I want to speak of you   I hear myself

not the track not the path
narrower higher
through something right behind you that
rises re turns
to this minute the twig knocked by the shoe

only for a fraction
for a few round gilded letters

up there our path
down there our path
we walk together through the great chain of mountains
farther down chipped stones
farthest down plants

gentian
the invincible sapphire of this word

we run: a quick drop down the dark leaf

dziś jest to co mówiłeś będzie
znów moje nie ma
na twoje znów jest
staram się żeby nasze było

było

zapamiętaj to, wymaluj wykrzycz

today is what you said would be
again it's not my own
you have it again your way
I'm trying hard if only ours was

was

remember it, paint shout out

nasze teraz pisane dużą literą
wyprawa po najdalej w rozpadlinę lata
kawałek słońca na liściu chwycony mimo woli
ach te słowa pierwsze z brzegu, mimo woli, „wolne złote"
nasze jestem na skraju trawnika
wibrujące dotknięcie ręki „tak głęboko"
myślisz studnia i już swoim językiem dajesz jej lustro

zamykasz oczy
ono będzie patrzyło

our now spelt with a capital letter
quest for the furthest into the rift of summer
a piece of sun on a leaf caught against our will
those random words, any will do, 'free golden'
our am on the verge of the lawn
vibrating touch of the hand 'so deep'
you think a well and your tongue gives it a lustre

you close your eyes
it will look

przez którą widzi
której nie widzi
która jest
z tego hen przed nami
co się otwiera każdemu inną, inaczej zieloną łąką
(czy zielono być trawą?)
szklarka, to spotkanie do zachwytu
do nie chwycenia

twój dziecinny latawiec
przezroczystą bibułką sfruwa mi w rękę

thanks to her whom he can see
whom he cannot see
who is
from this far far away before us
that opens for everyone into a different, differently green, meadow
(does it feel green to be grass?)
a brilliant emerald, this encounter to our rapture
not to be captured

your childlike kite
its see-through tissue flutters into my hand

nałożenia

nie ma na jest

jest na będzie

przedchwila na chwilę

przesunięcia

o łzę o nic o jeden wiersz

sprzed ciebie dziecko, sprzed wojny, sprzed siebie tej co tu siedzi na ławce z rzeką za plecami, sprzed tego cykania świerszcza

przezroczyste w przezroczystym

overlaps

what isn't with what is

what is with what will be

a pre-while with a while

shifts

by one teardrop nothing one poem

before you my child, before the war, before myself here on this bench with the river behind my back, before this chirping of the cricket

the see-through within the see-through

z czego zrobić gwiazdę
jasno dotknięte, ciemno powiedziane
zanim jest jest
jest nie ma

roześmiać się, wzruszyć ramionami
tak rozłożyć ręce

how to make a star
brighter touched, darker said
before there it is is
is is not

to laugh out, shrug your shoulders
spread your arms just so

cisza
nie ma słów na las w śniegu

brnąć w to dalej?
przystanąć?
uklęknąć?
zawrócić?

silence
no words for the woods in snow

to blunder into it farther?
pause?
kneel down?
turn back?

Te zapisy. No takie są, nie takie jakbym chciała. Zawsze słabsze od tego co właśnie jest. Wloką się latami, nie mogą zdążyć.

Niegotowe, niecałe, pełno w nich dziur (gdyby chociaż świeciły pustkami). Nie potrafię zagadać tych dziur. Moja wina, nie umiem. I nawet tego, czego nie umiem, nie umiem powiedzieć.

Gdyby ktoś przeczytał to niezapisane i to zapisane. Gdyby te rozrzucone kawałki po swojemu połączył. Gdyby ktokolwiek jakkolwiek zechciał to sobie

These writings. Well, that's what they are, not what I'd like them to be. All the time weaker than that which exists. They drag on for years, fail to keep pace.

Not ready, not complete, full of holes (if only their emptiness shone). I can't talk these holes away. My fault, I don't know how. I don't even know how to say that I don't know how.

If someone read the unwritten and the written. If these disparate pieces were put together in some personal manner. If only someone wanted to somehow

jest ciszy w pokoju
jest ścian, każdej inne
jest słońca na firanie
szarzejące jest kurzu
przez cienkie jest szyby
jest wróbla za oknem
jest dziecka po trawie, goniące motyla
jest motyla w siatce
płynące jest chmury

i znowu: jestem

w tym ogromnym
kolistym kulistym nieczyimś
rozdziawionym zajadłym parzącym
trawomocnym śmigłoskrzydłym biegłonogim
cieknącym zaciekłym
dotkliwym
jest

the is of the silence in the room
the is of the walls, each so different
the is of the sunshine on the curtain
the greying is of the dust
through the thin is of the glass
the is of the sparrow outside the window
the is of the child on the grass, chasing a butterfly
the is of the butterfly in the net
the floating is of the cloud

and once again: I am

in this vast
circular spherical nobody's
agape virulent scorching
grass-strong swift-winged quick-legged
dripping rabid
acute
is

może tylko nie ma komu powiedzieć siebie głośno z tymi od kiedy pamięta zacięciami w najbardziej nieoczekiwanych miejscach w tym samym zawsze oczekiwanym momencie?

bo kto to wytrzyma nawet gdyby się znalazł cierpliwszy od stołu?

powiedzieć czy powierzyć choćby same początki czegoś ważnego (odkrycia mniejsze chowa w tyle głowy)

zwłaszcza zależy jej na oczach i twarzach, na uśmiechu rozumienia w czymś podobnym kimś podobnym

… jej niedorozmowy, siedzi podparta obiema rękami o brzeg stołu i wygląda że śpi, dziś tylko kupiła pęczek kopru

maybe she has no one to say herself to loud enough with this long-recalled stutter in the most unexpected places in the same well expected moment?

and how to stand it even if someone was more patient than a table?

to say or to vouchsafe at least the beginnings of something vital (she hides minor discoveries at the back of her head)

she is particularly keen on the eyes and the faces   the smile of comprehension in something similar someone similar

… her inconversations   she sits with both her hands on the edge of the table   seems to be asleep   today she has only bought one bunch of dill

moje dziecko – w Twoim brzuchu
Twoja twarz – w mojej wiśle

ciekniesz mi przez palce do morza
i nie umiem się napić

... nieba od ziemi
ziarna od plew
bólu od bólu
ciebie ode mnie
ciała od kości

baranku gołąbku synku przyjacielu!

my child – in your belly
your face – in my Vistula

you drip through my fingers into the sea
and I do not know how to drink

... heaven from earth
the wheat from the chaff
the pain from the pain
you from me
flesh from bone

my little lamb bird son friend!

a ja w tym chodzę chodzę i podlewam kwiaty
oddycham, gdy świat wstrzymał oddech

o tyle śmierci żywsza

o mnie ze mną? o ciebie do mnie? o mnie do ciebie? bliżej?
o nią w świecie? o świat w niej? sam świat?
o dom? o drzewo? o syna?
i o to zapisane? o Ty zapisane w pośpiechu?
o nam pisane jutro?

jutro, bądź łagodne!

    and I walk in this
           walk and water the plants
                breathe when the world has held its breath

that much more alive to death

        of me together with me? of you to me? of me to you? closer?
        of her in the world? of the world in her? world itself?
        of the house? the tree? the son?
        of what has been written? of You written in haste?
        of our fate-written tomorrow?

        tomorrow, be gentle!

obieram kartofle, głaszczę cię po głowie, podnoszę listek z ziemi, zapalam światło, zapalam papierosa, chwytam klamkę, wyjmuję bilet tramwajowy

nie spiesz się tak, za prędko siwiejesz

biegnij biegnij, tyle twojego co zakłuje w piersiach

I peel potatoes, stroke your head, pick a leaf
off the ground, light a lamp, light a cigarette, turn the knob,
take a tram ticket out

don't hurry so, you're turning grey too fast

run run, that much is yours: stabs in your chest

najprędzej gubię czasowniki, zostają rzeczowniki, rzeczy
już tylko zaimki osobowe (dużo ja, coraz więcej ja)
a imiona? giną, spójniki giną
trzy słowa, dwa słowa
wreszcie mój, mój we mnie
mój ze mną
świat

ja w pierwszej i ostatniej osobie

I lose verbs quickest, nouns, things remain
now only personal pronouns (lots of I, more and more I)
and names? lost, conjunctions lost
three words, two words
finally my – mine in me
mine with me –
world

I in the first and last person

dałem ci ręce a nie uniosłaś mnie wyżej (?)
dałem ci uszy a nie słyszałaś (?)
dałem ci usta a mówiłaś za dużo (?)
dałem ci oczy

światło, w którym nikogo nie rozpoznaję

I gave you hands yet you didn't lift me higher (?)
I gave you ears yet you didn't hear (?)
I gave you lips yet you spoke too much (?)
I gave you eyes

light by which I recognize nobody

ich świecenie, mój podziw (?)
ich śmierć, moje złoto (?)
z nich cała (?)
to co budzi prowadzi (?) szeleści (?)

dziecinnie zielone krótkie zdyszane oziminy

their glitter, my awe (?)
their death, my gold (?)
me of them (?)
that which awakens leads (?) rustles (?)

childishly green short breathless winter wheat

ciągle ta sama nieopowiadalność!
(świecenie świata, szarość papieru)

światło papieru, kolor tej szarości

labirynt – w którym tylko każdy z osobna szczegół może być nazwany

yet again the same can't-describe!
(the glow of the world, the grey of paper)

the shine of the paper, the hue of this grey

labyrinth – where only an individual detail may be named

park mówił sam za siebie
każde w swoim i bez jak

po tej i po tamtej stronie szyby
ale nie ma szyby i nie ma stron

the park spoke for itself
each in their and without how

on this and the other side of the glass
except there's no glass and there are no sides

mamy siebie krótko na wieczne zdziwienie
patrz uważnie, przed tobą nie oddany uśmiech
(ta twarz z bliska, szeroko rozstawione oczy)

we have each other briefly for eternal wonder
look closely, right before you an unrequited smile
(the face so near, the wide-set eyes)

dokładnie czoło, dokładnie usta, dokładnie dłonie
z tą samą brudną plamką przy paznokciu

z warkoczykami
w żorżetowej sukience
z dalią przy policzku, truskawką do buzi
w tamtej błękitnoszarej przepasce na włosach

(i: czy popiół zakwita?)

exactly the forehead, exactly the lips, exactly the hands
with the same dirty stain at the fingernail

with little plaits
in a georgette dress
with a dahlia at the cheek, a strawberry to the mouth
in that blue-grey band in the hair

(and: would ashes bloom?)

kocham cię razem z twoją śmiercią

I love you together with your death

trzy sny o ojcu odkładam na później
może się przydadzą

to już stara łza, automatyczna
zawsze znajdę ją w tym samym miejscu

the three dreams about my father
I put them aside for later
they may still come in handy

that's already an old tear, automatic
I find it always at the same spot

tyle waży tyle mierzy tyle podobny tyle cudowny tyle ja
tyle tych ciemnych włosków

„jesteś moim będzie"

każde słowo w razie potrzeby może być zdobyczą

that much weight that much tall that much
similar that much wonderful that
much me that much dark hair

'you are my will-be'

when in need every word turns into a trophy

wypadł ci pierwszy mleczny ząb
i już tym pierwszym odgryzasz się ode mnie

już się nie spotkamy
ja mówię mleko, ty mówisz biel

... nieba od ziemi
ziarna od plew
bólu od bólu
ciebie ode mnie
ciała od kości

wżarty we mnie znak dzielenia

your first milk tooth's just fallen out
and you're biting apart from me now

now we cannot get together again
I say milk, you say white

                … heaven from earth
                the wheat from the chaff
                the pain from the pain
                you from me
                flesh from bone

                gnawed deep into me, the division sign

przebudzenie, jedno od paru miesięcy żywe

znowu dajemy sobie krzyki życia strącamy talerze, już ledwo starcza mi ciała na te rany

kolejna wiosna pod nogami budzi fiołki, tyle urodzin tyle początków, szepczemy fiołki

i jeszcze jedno przebudzenie, jeszcze to ostatnie urodzenie

wypluć wszystko

awakening   in the last couple of months the first alive

again we're exchanging screams of life knocking off the plates   I hardly have enough flesh for these wounds

another spring wakes violets under our feet   so many births so many beginnings   we whisper violets

and one more awakening   one last birth

to spit it all out

rozbierz się z Krystyny
z dziecka matki kobiety
lokatorki kochanki turystki żony

zostaje rozbieranie
smugi zrzucanych ubrań
lekkie ruchy, nic więcej

strip yourself of Krystyna
of child mother woman
lodger lover tourist wife

what's left is undressing
trails of discarded clothes
light gestures, nothing more

jestem do znikania

chcę niczym świadczyć
niczego wziąć niczego mieć
nikogo zatrzymać

i te żal się Boże podróże
żeby mnie było więcej
żeby mi się dużo widziało

jestem wszystkim czego nie mam
furtką bez ogrodu

I am for vanishing

I want to give testimony
with nothing to take
nothing to have
nothing nobody
to keep

and those God knows journeys
to make me more
to make me see a great deal

I am everything I have not
gate without its garden

mieszkanie

niemieszkanie

powiew

powietrze które mną oddycha

wiatr dotknięty mokrym palcem

dwelling

nondwelling

breeze

air that breathes me

wind touched with the wet finger

pisz pisz aż w pisaniu znikniesz

patrz patrz aż znikniesz w patrzeniu

write write on till you vanish in writing

look look on till you vanish in looking

w zielono kulisto wysoko ostro

no mów

w odświętnie, wesoło, uroczyście

no mów

w radośnie, podniośle

no mów

w zbawczo

mów

into the green high spherical sharp

go on, speak

into the festive, cheerful, ceremonial

go on, speak

into the joyous, elevated

go on, speak

into the redemptive

speak

jest rosnące drzewem

jest płynące

jest biegnące, jest latające

jest od początku

jest nie tak

jest nie to, jest do końca

jest nie ma, jest jest

jest – jestem

świat z Tobą

the is growing into a tree

the is flowing

the is running, the is flying

the is from the beginning

the is not what it should be

the is not the one, the is to the end

the is there is not, the is there is

the is – I am

the world with You

że jesteś w rozłożystym powietrzu
otulona w chmury

(otulające cię chmury)

(chmury)

                                          drzewo tak drzewo
                                        że drzewa już nie ma

                                        chmury (chmury)

that you are in the wide branching air
wrapped by clouds

(clouds wrapping you)

(clouds)

                                the tree yes the tree
                                that the tree is no more

                                clouds (clouds)

próbowałam siebie powiedzieć całym lasem

chciało się powiedzieć synem, wnukiem

mówiło siebie słońcem, wiatrem

chmurą

        mówiąc milczę

        mycie szklanek, patrzenie pod światło

        wrześniowe niebo i te chmury przejrzyste

I tried to say myself with all the forest

one tended to speak through the son and grandson

one used to say oneself through the sun, the wind

the cloud

                speaking I'm silent

                the washing of glasses, the looking against the light

                September sky and these clouds so see-through

dróżki w ogrodzie

(czarne wgłąb)

(przeskoki, zgłębienia)

dom przed zniknięciem w drzewach

dom znikający w drzewach

paths in the garden

(black deep inside)

(leaps, deep insights)

the house before it vanishes among the trees

the house vanishing among the trees

ach, to szukanie
– po cichutku po morzach po górach po nie

ja
– to samo co ten świerk ten śnieg ten ukos

gubienie po drodze
– a to pole, a to się, a to siebie, a to kurz

ty
– a to kto tam?

                                        oddziel jasne od słońca

                                        biegnie od drogi

                                        twoje od moje

                                        moje od?

ah, this searching
– on tiptoe on seas on mountains on no

me
– same as this spruce this snow this slant

the losing along the way
– once a field, once itself, once myself, once dust

you
– and who is it there?

                                      separate bright from the sun

                                      runs from the road

                                      yours from mine

                                      mine from?

nie pomyśleć nic

strach pomyśleć nic

bliżej tych co poszli

blisko tych których tu już nie ma

blisko tych do których mi coraz bliżej

not to think nothing

dread to think nothing

closer to those who have gone

close to those who are no longer here

close to those to whom I'm closer and closer

w oczy temu, w twarz, w liście

piasek

into the eyes of the, into the face, into the leaves

sand

piasek

miasta, domy, ogrody, ścieżki, liście, rzeki, jeziora, bajora, morze, mewy, lasy, jelenie, sarny, konie, koty, psy, łapy, chrapy, brzuchy, włosy

moje włosy, moje brwi, moje rzęsy, moje oczy, moje łzy, moje usta, piasek

sand

towns, houses, gardens, paths, leaves, rivers, lakes, swamps, sea, gulls, forests, stags, fawns, horses, cats, dogs, paws, nostrils, bellies, hair

my hair, my brows, my lashes, my eyes, my tears,
my mouth, sand

rzeczowniki, czasowniki, przydawki, pierwiastki, dopełnienia, tryby mowy, imiesłowy, przymiotniki, sylaby, fonemy

moja dykcja, mój głos, moje wargi, mój nos, moje czoło, moje oczy, moje usta, piasek

piasek

nouns, verbs, attributes, roots,
objects, moods of speech, participles, adjectives,
syllables, phonemes

my diction, my voice, my lips, my nose, my forehead,
my eyes, my mouth, sand

sand

mów!

speak!

Jestem. Współżywa, współczynna, współwinna. Współzielona, współdrzewna. Współistnieję. Ty jeszcze nie wiesz co to znaczy. Obdarowana przenikaniem. Znikam jestem. Współtrwam (z Tobą) w tym szklistym dniu (z tym szklistym dniem w którym znikam) który znika ze mną tak lekko. Nie wiem co to znaczy. Współotwarta z oknem, współpłynna z rzeką. Jestem żeby wiedzieć znikam? Znikam żeby wiedzieć jestem? Cała ale całej nigdzie nie ma. Współprzelatująca, współniebna. Pół wieku żyłam po to!

I am. Co-alive, co-active, co-guilty. Co-green, co-tree. I co-exist. You do not know yet what it means. Gifted with diffusion. I vanish I am. I co-endure (with You) on this glassy day (with this glassy day into which I vanish) which vanishes with me so lightly. I don't know what it means. Co-open with the window, co-flowing with the river. I am in order to know I vanish? I vanish in order to know I am? All of me but all of me nowhere to be found. Co-fleeting, co-skyward. Half a century I have lived for this!

BIOGRAPHICAL NOTES

KRYSTYNA MIŁOBĘDZKA was born in Margonin, Poland, in 1932. She has written plays for children, which are collected in *Siała baba mak* [A Pocket Full of Posies, 1995]. As a scholar of children's theatre, she has published the monograph *Teatr Jana Dormana* [Jan Dorman's Theatre, 1990] and the volume of essays *W widnokręgu Odmieńca* [In the Misfit's Circumference, 2008]. She is the author of twelve books of poetry: *Anaglify* [Anaglyphs, 1960], *Pokrewne* [Of Kin, 1970], *Dom, pokarmy* [Home, Foods, 1975], *Wykaz treści* [Register of Contents, 1984], *Pamiętam (zapisy stanu wojennego* [I Remember (Writings Under Martial Law), 1992], *Przed wierszem. Zapisy dawne i nowe* [Before the Poem: Writings Old and New, 1994], *Imiesłowy* [Participles, 2000], *Wszystkowiersze* [Omnipoems, 2000], *Przesuwanka* [Shifting Rhyme, 2003], *Po krzyku* [After a Shout, 2004], *gubione* [one by one lost, 2008] and *dwanaście wierszy w kolorze* [twelve poems in colour, 2012]. Her collected *Zbierane. 1960-2005* [Gathered. 1960-2005] appeared in 2006, and *zbierane, gubione* [gathered, lost] in 2010. Recipient of numerous awards, she was nominated for the NIKE Prize in 2006 and won the Silesius Award in 2009. In 2013 she was awarded the Silesius for Lifetime Achievement. She lives in Puszczykowo near Poznań.

ELŻBIETA WÓJCIK-LEESE translates contemporary Polish poetry into English. Her translations appear regularly in journals and anthologies, such as *New European Poets* (Graywolf Press, 2008), *Six Polish Poets* (Arc Publications, 2009) and *the Ecco Anthology of International Poetry* (Ecco, 2010). In 2011 her versions featured on the London Underground. *Salt Monody* is her selection from Marzanna Kielar (Zephyr Press, 2006). She co-edited *Carnivorous Boy Carnivorous Bird: Poetry from Poland* (Zephyr Press, 2004), which presents twenty-four Polish poets born between

1958 and 1969. She co-edits peer-reviewed *Przekładaniec: A Journal of Literary Translation A Journal of Literary Translation* (Kraków, Poland). She also translates Polish children's books and English-language poetry. As a translator and writer, she has been involved in the *Metropoetica* project, *Poetry and Urban Space: Women Writing Cities* (www.metropoetica.org; Seren, 2013). As a Fulbright scholar, she examined Elizabeth Bishop's archives, which resulted in *Cognitive Poetic Readings in Elizabeth Bishop: Portrait of a Mind Thinking* (Mouton de Gruyter, 2010). She lives in Copenhagen.

Robert Minhinnick was born in 1952 and lives in south Wales. He has published nine collections of poetry, including *The Adulterer's Tongue: Six Contemporary Welsh Poets* (Carcanet, 2003) and *New Selected Poems* (Carcanet, 2012). He has been the winner of a Society of Authors Eric Gregory Award and a Cholmondeley Award, and has twice won the Forward Prize for best individual poem. His books of essays have twice won the Wales Book of the Year Prize. His first novel, *Sea Holly*, was published by Seren in 2007. Robert Minhinnick edited *Poetry Wales* magazine from 1997 to 2008. He co-founded Friends of the Earth (Cymru) and Sustainable Wales, and is an advisor to Sustainable Wales. His collection of prose, *Island of Lightning*, appears from Seren in late 2013.

Also available in the Arc Publications
'VISIBLE POETS' SERIES (Series Editor: Jean Boase-Beier)

No. 1 – MIKLÓS RADNÓTI (Hungary)
Camp Notebook
Translated by Francis Jones, introduced by George Szirtes

No. 2 – BARTOLO CATTAFI (Italy)
Anthracite
Translated by Brian Cole, introduced by Peter Dale
(Poetry Book Society Recommended Translation)

No. 3 – MICHAEL STRUNGE (Denmark)
A Virgin from a Chilly Decade
Translated by Bente Elsworth, introduced by John Fletcher

No. 4 – TADEUSZ RÓŻEWICZ (Poland)
recycling
Translated by Barbara Bogoczek (Plebanek) & Tony Howard,
introduced by Adam Czerniawski

No. 5 – CLAUDE DE BURINE (France)
Words Have Frozen Over
Translated by Martin Sorrell, introduced by Susan Wicks

No. 6 – CEVAT ÇAPAN (Turkey)
Where Are You, Susie Petschek?
Translated by Cevat Çapan & Michael Hulse,
introduced by A. S. Byatt

No. 7 – JEAN CASSOU (France)
33 Sonnets of the Resistance
With an original introduction by Louis Aragon
Translated by Timothy Adès, introduced by Alistair Elliot

No. 8 – ARJEN DUINKER (Holland)
The Sublime Song of a Maybe
Translated by Willem Groenewegen, introduced by Jeffrey Wainwright

No. 9 – MILA HAUGOVÁ (Slovakia)
Scent of the Unseen
Translated by James & Viera Sutherland-Smith,
introduced by Fiona Sampson

No. 10 – ERNST MEISTER (Germany)
Between Nothing and Nothing
Translated by Jean Boase-Beier, introduced by John Hartley Williams

No. 11 – YANNIS KONDOS (Greece)
Absurd Athlete
Translated by David Connolly, introduced by David Constantine

No. 12 – BEJAN MATUR (Turkey)
In the Temple of a Patient God
Translated by Ruth Christie, introduced by Maureen Freely

No. 13 – GABRIEL FERRATER (Catalonia / Spain)
Women and Days
Translated by Arthur Terry, introduced by Seamus Heaney

No. 14 – INNA LISNIANSKAYA (Russia)
Far from Sodom
Translated by Daniel Weissbort, introduced by Elaine Feinstein
(Poetry Book Society Recommended Translation)

No. 15 – SABINE LANGE (Germany)
The Fishermen Sleep
Translated by Jenny Williams, introduced by Mary O'Donnell

No. 16 – TAKAHASHI MUTSUO (Japan)
We of Zipangu
Translated by James Kirkup & Tamaki Makoto,
introduced by Glyn Pursglove

No. 17 – JURIS KRONBERGS (Latvia)
Wolf One-Eye
Translated by Mara Rozitis, introduced by Jaan Kaplinski

No. 18 – REMCO CAMPERT (Holland)
I Dreamed in the Cities at Night
Translated by Donald Gardner, introduced by Paul Vincent

No. 19 – DOROTHEA ROSA HERLIANY (Indonesia)
Kill the Radio
Translated by Harry Aveling, introduced by Linda France

No. 20 – SOLEÏMAN ADEL GUÉMAR (Algeria)
State of Emergency
Translated by Tom Cheesman & John Goodby,
introduced by Lisa Appignanesi
(PEN Translation Award)

No. 21 – ELI TOLARETXIPI (Spain / Basque)
Still Life with Loops
Translated by Philip Jenkins, introduced by Robert Crawford

No. 22 – FERNANDO KOFMAN (Argentina)
The Flights of Zarza
Translated by Ian Taylor, introduced by Andrew Graham Yooll

No. 23 – LARISSA MILLER (Russia)
Guests of Eternity
Translated by Richard McKane, introduced by Sasha Dugdale
(Poetry Book Society Recommended Translation)

No. 24 – ANISE KOLTZ (Luxembourg)
At the Edge of Night
Translated by Anne-Marie Glasheen, introduced by Caroline Price

No. 25 – MAURICE CARÊME (Belgium)
Defying Fate
Translated by Christopher Pilling, introduced by Martin Sorrell

No. 26 – VALÉRIE ROUZEAU (France)
Cold Spring in Winter
Translated by Susan Wicks, introduced by Stephen Romer
(Short-listed, Griffin Poetry Prize, 2010 &
Oxford-Weidenfeld Translation Prize, 2010)

No. 27 – RAZMIK DAVOYAN (France)
Whispers and Breath of the Meadows
Translated by Arminé Tamrazian, introduced by W. N. Herbert

No. 28 – FRANÇOIS JACQMIN (Belgium)
The Book of the Snow
Translated by Philip Mosley, introduced by Clive Scott
(Short-listed, Griffin Poetry Prize, 2011)

No. 29 – KRISTIINA EHIN (Estonia)
The Scent of Your Shadow
Translated by Ilmar Lehtpere, introduced by Sujata Bhatt
(Poetry Book Society Recommended Translation)

No. 30 – META KUŠAR (Slovenia)
Ljubljana
Translated by Ana Jelnikar & Stephen Watts,
introduced by Francis R. Jones

No. 31 – LUDWIG STEINHERR (Germany)
Before the Invention of Paradise
Translated by Richard Dove, introduced by Jean Boase-Beier

No. 32 – FABIO PUSTERLA (Switzerland)
Days Full of Caves and Tigers
Translated by Simon Knight, introduced by Alan Brownjohn

No. 33 – LEV LOSEFF (Russia)
As I Said
Translated by G.S. Smith, introduced by Barry P. Scherr

No. 34 – ANTONIO MOURA (Brazil)
Silence River
Translated by Stefan Tobler, introduced by David Treece

No. 35 – Birhan Keskin (Turkey)
& Silk & Love & Flame
Translated by George Messo, introduced by Amanda Dalton

No. 36 – Cheran (Tamil / Sri Lanka)
In a Time of Burning
Translated by Lakshmi Holmström, introduced by Sascha Ebeling